THE RUSHOLME SKETCHER BY LEN GRANT

The Rusholme Sketcher first appeared online at: www.therusholmesketcher.co.uk

I'm a Manchester-based photographer, writer and sketcher. Check out nearly three decades of storytelling at www.lengrant.co.uk

Further copies of this book are available from my website and all good Manchester bookshops

On Twitter and Instagram I'm len_grant

"One minute one shop closes and the next minute another opens. It's like life, always changing."

Ibrahim, Rusholme window cleaner

THE STRIP

We'd race out of the classroom on the bell and sprint down Thurlow Street, hoping to catch a 53 bus that would get us to Belle Vue train station for the 16.09.

Maybe because I was always running, my recollection of Wilmslow Road in the 1970s is sketchy. I remember the post office and the sweet shop that would sell single cigarettes to us under-age schoolboys. Now they are Gelato Passion and Lal Qila respectively.

In my haste, I didn't notice that towards the end of that decade this small suburb three miles out of town was slowly changing. New migrants from south Asia were made welcome as they established their restaurants, fashion houses, jewellers and greengrocers.

The restaurants and sweet houses became popular with the local population and, before long, this quarter mile strip of the A6010 became known as the Curry Mile. It even had its own branding.

"During that period business was booming, it was fantastic," one restaurant veteran told me recently. "Everyone was happy. In the last ten years things have started to change. Nowadays you can easily have meals delivered to your home or buy cheap curries from the supermarket. But restaurants will survive as long as they offer something new."

Rusholme itself has changed again as it reflects international migration. Catering for a Middle Eastern clientele, the 'strip' has seen a proliferation of shisha bars and shawarma kebab takeaways, with a dozen or more barber shops thrown in.

Skip drivers and signage contractors continue to be kept busy as premises change hands at an alarming rate. Rusholme evolves faster perhaps than anywhere else in the city. An ideal subject for storytelling, then.

As well as being a day-to-day destination to share a shisha pipe or buy fresh jalebi, Rusholme also serves as a venue for celebration. The pavements become even more animated during Eid festivals and national celebrations with the roads grinding to gridlock. For a community too frequently under fire in an increasingly intolerant Britain, this place remains somewhere in which to celebrate and feel at ease.

My own sketching journey is, so far, relatively short. I became an urban sketcher in 2013 [see www.urbansketchers.org] and have added sketching into my professional portfolio along with photography. The Rusholme Sketcher started as a blog and is a personal project that demonstrates the potential of telling stories with words and sketches.

Although brimming with sketching potential, the Curry Mile wasn't originally obvious to me as a subject for this project. Rusholme is so close to home that the familiar had become invisible. Yes, I'd sketched here before, but only from one of its three benches with a view across towards Eastern Gold and the Kurdish Barbers.

The Rusholme Sketcher started one Friday morning when I cycled down the road towards town. Stopping at traffic lights, the idea suddenly dawned. I immediately pedalled back to the familiar barbers and asked if I could sit on the sofa and draw their salon. Harry, the barber closest to the door, said I was welcome and my project began.

Len Grant
Rusholme
November 2018

"There seem to be loads of barbers in Rusholme," I say.
"Fourteen," he says. "I've counted them all."
"And is there enough work for you all?"
"We're all pretty busy. I've got customers from London,
Birmingham and Leeds who come to Rusholme for
a hair cut."
　　　"A double zero on top and a number one for
　　　　the beard," says Harry's next customer.
　　　　　There's not a pair of scissors in sight
　　　　　　and the top of the head doesn't take
　　　　　　　long. For the next 15 minutes Harry works
　　　　　　　　intently on the beard, like a sculptor refining his
　　　　　　　　　masterpiece.

I'm upstairs at the Afghan Cuisine Café. "Wow!" says a customer looking over my shoulder. Turns out he works at the Amazon distribution centre near the airport and comes here to eat every Friday on his day off.

When I'm finished I take my book downstairs to show Matiola and ask if I can chat between customers.

"What's your most popular dish?"

Matiola looks up at the menu above the counter. "I'd say qabily pulao."

I must have looked quizzical because he explains: "Rice and lamb, and then carrots and raisins. The rice is cooked in the soup of the lamb and then the carrots and raisins go on top."

"Is it someone's signature dish?"

"We have one guy in the back and he basically makes qabily pulao every day and then goes home."

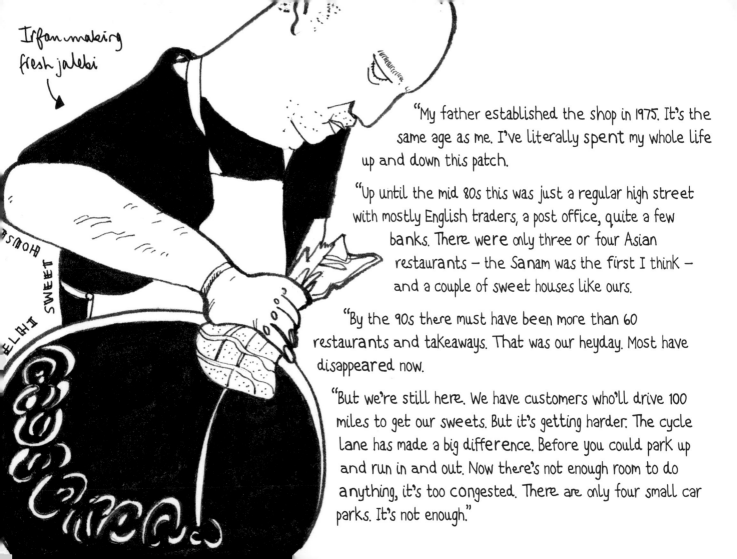

Irfan making
fresh jalebi

DELHI SWEET HOUSE

"My father established the shop in 1975. It's the same age as me. I've literally spent my whole life up and down this patch.

"Up until the mid 80s this was just a regular high street with mostly English traders, a post office, quite a few banks. There were only three or four Asian restaurants – the Sanam was the first I think – and a couple of sweet houses like ours.

"By the 90s there must have been more than 60 restaurants and takeaways. That was our heyday. Most have disappeared now.

"But we're still here. We have customers who'll drive 100 miles to get our sweets. But it's getting harder. The cycle lane has made a big difference. Before you could park up and run in and out. Now there's not enough room to do anything, it's too congested. There are only four small car parks. It's not enough."

It says above the door that the Chippy was established in 1977. "It hasn't changed much," says Bakhdyar as he cleans the tables around me.

"And I'm guessing you don't do much fish and chips. What do you sell most of?"

"Kobeda Kebab," he says, pointing out dozens of metal skewers hanging in a fridge. "We'll sell 200-250 of those tonight."

As I'm finishing my watercolour three men come in, one of them clearly very excited. "We've just driven up from London. This is our first stop in Manchester," he says, greeting Bakhdyar as if he were a close friend. "My mouth is literally watering. I'm craving this food."

"What have you ordered?" I ask.

"The classic kobeda, which is what the Rusholme Chippy is known for. A 5-star rating is too low for this place."

"And you can't find anything like this in London?"

"To be honest with you," he says, handing over his cash, "I can't find anything like this in the world."

It's been quiet until now., but as I finish the line work the car park slowly fills.

An older man with resplendent white beard and matching skullcap tells me he's been praying here since 1965.

"I was 22 and back then it was an old Victorian building which got knocked down and replaced with this." He waves a hand at the Central Mosque. "It's been extended since then. For Friday prayers we regularly get over 1,500."

"Is there a prayer service about to start?" I ask as a taxi pulls up.

"Yes, quarter to two. I come and pray most days," he says, making his way to the entrance.

On the TV behind me, the Al Jazeera sports channel is starting their coverage of the Burnley and Manchester United game. The studio is in Qatar but the match is being played 25 miles north of here at Turf Moor.

The Kurdistan Restaurant fills. Plates of lamb quzy, Kurdish Kebab and huge breads are brought to the plastic-covered tables. Everyone knows the drill. I suspect I'm the only one who hasn't been here before.

I understand nothing the commentator says but, even with my back to the TV, have a good idea how the game is going. He's biased, or United are completely dominating the first half. "Lingard... Pogba... Ashley Young..."

There's no mention of a Burnley player.

Ten minutes to go. United are one up. The commentator has stopped trying to describe the match with actual words. "Oi... Oi... Oi... Mata," he shouts as if he's riding a rollercoaster. "Oi... Oi... Oi... Rashford."

My sketch finished, I leave during extra time.

It's just warm enough to sit out today. I've brought my little stool which I set up opposite Jaffa, the popular Mediterranean café.

A Tesco delivery van narrowly misses two rollerskaters on the cycle path as a bearded man in a wooly Man United hat stops by. "I'm not being nosey or anything," he says.

"No, it's fine," I say by way of reassurance. "Come and have a look."

He steps closer. "That's not a bad piece of work. Good luck to you lad," he says before he takes up his position outside Jaffa with his Café Nero cup in hand.

Everyone seems to be ignoring the match until Young scores. Cheers erupt around the Antalya and, through the plastic partition, from a noisy crowd in the café next door.

Five minutes later he does it again. I look up in time to see him sliding across the turf on his knees. The customers cheer again but are quickly back to their sisha pipes, kebabs and chatter. Salah's charcoal pan goes from table to table.

Seventy minutes gone and Watford pull two back, one after the other. It's 2-3 and now people start to take notice. But just before the final whistle United's Jesse Lingard puts a comeback out of reach and everyone relaxes.

"It's 25 years since Cantona signed for United and there's a very Cantona-esque celebration from Lingard," says the commentator.

"We make them all upstairs in our own kitchens," Dora tells me. I make a mental note to come back and ask to draw the chefs at work.

When I do, the Pastry House is cordoned off and gutted. "There was a fire the other week," says the man folding sheets in the laundry next door, "it'll re-open in a couple of months."

Rusholme. Always changing.

"There's something quite Zen about wheel building," says Adrian, as he fits another spoke. "I think if I was cast onto a desert island I'd be happy as long as I had a wheel and a spoke key. I'd be constantly taking it apart and rebuilding it again."

I'm upstairs at Bicycle Doctor, the cycling co-operative that's been a Rusholme institution since 1983.

Having finished the day's repairs Adrian is doing some work on his own fixed gear bike, cobbled together from unwanted bits and bobs from the workshop.

Of course, as a serious cyclist, it's not his only bike. As well as his 'flagship' road bike – and a mountain bike that rarely sees mountains – he tells me he uses a sit-up-and-beg Dutch-style bike he found in the shed. "It belongs to my landlord's niece but he doesn't mind me using it."

"It's very quiet today," I say to one of the barbers sitting outside his empty salon.

"It's Ramadan," he says. "Everywhere will be open again this evening," he puts two fingers and a thumb up to his mouth, "for something to eat when they break their fast."

Between customers Mariam and Zulfiqar have been watching as my sketch of their store progresses. "It looks good in black and white," says Mariam, "but I think people will recognise it more with colour."

When I'm done she takes some photographs for Instagram and I open the voice recorder on my phone. "So the shop is called Junaid Jamshed by Janan," I say, "and you'd say it's the equivalent of perhaps Monsoon in the UK?"

"In Pakistan there are over 60 stores," says Zulfiqar, "and there are branches all over the world: in Australia, in the US. So, yes, we'd be a bit like Monsoon I'd guess."

"Don't forget to tag me," I joke with Mariam. "And Junaid is a fashion designer?"

"He was a well-known singer in Pakistan in the early 80s," explains Zulfiqar. "He had a group called Vital Signs and they had some really big hits. For maybe 20 years he was on top of the charts. When he stopped singing he turned to charity work and also started a clothing brand."

"A bit like Victoria Beckham?" I suggest. "She went into fashion after being a Spice Girl."

"Oh yes," says Zulfiqar, "I remember watching them in a Fallowfield pub once, when they were just starting up. I just happened to be there. Then I saw them again switching on the lights in Oxford Street. So, yes, a bit like Victoria Beckham."

"Does he still do a lot for charity?" I ask.

"Unfortunately he passed away in an air crash in December 2016. He was a very humble guy, very humble. We knew him personally. A really nice guy, dedicated to good causes."

There's some last minute shopping before the big day. This is the equivalent of Christmas Eve.

Rails of traditional clothes are pushed onto the pavements, not just outside the clothing shops but in every spare space.

Outside the derelict Huntsman pub the discounted fashions sit beside pallets of onions from the next door superstore. It's a bizarre juxtaposition. Even Ravi's have substituted some of their coriander and parsley with boxes of formal shirts and colourful bangles.

It's Eid al-Fitr, the breaking of the fast after Ramadan. There's a party mood in Rusholme, heightened in some of the shisha bars as Iran and Morocco play their World Cup opener.

Families stream up and down, all in their finest traditional clothes apart from the self-conscious teenagers who opt for a smart T-shirt and jeans.

As I draw I find myself in conversation with an older man looking over my shoulder. Turns out John is an artist originally from Iraq. He tells me my work reminds him of an old friend. "And you look a bit like Francis Bacon," he says, "but he was gay of course."

As late afternoon turns to early evening, the blaring vuvuzelas and the honking car horns become indistinguishable. I take refuge in one of the busy shisha bars where I drink mint tea and draw the scene.

Michelle the barmaid comes out to see how it's going. "So are you the last surviving pub in Rusholme?" I ask from my stool.

"The last bastion," she says.

We reminisce about the ones that have been lost: Hardy's Well, The Whitworth, The Welcome. We forget The Clarence on the other side of the strip, now a shisha bar. "I did some of my underage drinking in The Welcome," I say, "I think it's a dentist's now."

Haych and his older brother walk by as I'm sketching The Albert. "That's brilliant," he says. "Have you just drawn that?"

"What position do you play?" I ask, noticing his Reddish Vulcans kit.

"Centre forward," he says, tapping the number 10 on his shirt. "This is my brother, he plays for Manchester City Academy."

"And what position do you play?" I ask the brother.

"Centre mid."

"And who's better?" I ask, stirring it.

The older brother replies: "I'm faster but he's got the skills."

"So should I be getting your autographs before you're dead famous?"

"Tag me on Instagram," says Haych, "and I'll remember you."

The lads insist I draw them but aren't up for keeping still. "I'll take a photo," I say, "check it out on Instagram in the next day or so."

By way of explanation I pass one of my postcards to the two men closest to me. "Do you mind if you're in my drawing?" I ask.

The second looks from the postcard back up to me: "I follow you on Instagram!" says Hazaifa, "are you the actual bloke, the Rusholme Sketcher?" I sense some disappointment.

It's Portugal versus Iran, plus it's over 24 degrees, so the shisha bars are crammed. Every chair and pipe is called into service.

Until Portugal score just before half time I'm unsure of the crowd's allegiances but Quaresma's goal seems to divide the fans into two equal camps. The waiters could always double up as stewards.

The second half is punctuated by some bloke sprinting down the cycle lane towards Kansas Fried Chicken followed by half a dozen random men. Sensing a commotion half my subjects abandon their pipes and mint teas to follow. Whatever the fracas, it's quickly over and everyone settles back to watch Iran's goalie save a Ronaldo penalty. More hysteria.

In extra time the referee yet again refers to his VAR screen on the touchline before awarding Iran the penalty they score to level. In the final minute there is another Iranian goal — enough to knock Portugal out — but it's disallowed. Phew, what a scorcher.

S. KOREA 0-2 MEXICO

(and then S. Korea scored in extra time)

LAMB CHOPS FROM THE 80S

"I remember Sundays at Mughli were always family days and we'd all perch in that corner by the window. There's always something going on in this road and we'd pretty much spend the whole day people-watching.

"We'd have lunch here and when I was six or seven my brothers and I would get through a lot of lamb chops. We'd have six each to begin with and then another six.

"We'd be here for so long we'd have dinner here as well. Mum and dad would order something else from the kitchen but we'd break the family rules and get pizza from what is now the Al Jazeera café, and milkshakes from Moonlight."

"Can I help you?" asks the security guard as I eye up the construction site on the corner of Banff Road. It takes some explaining that the huge crane has caught my attention and I'm about to set my stool up on the pavement and draw the site.

The barber sitting outside his salon down the side street comes to take a look. Wesam says he'll be happy to see these 150 flats completed and the road open again. It's not doing his trade any good.

Next he brings seven-year-old Mohammed, the son of a friend. "You're good at drawing," says the boy. Within minutes, he's pulled a chair from the barber's and the two of us are sitting together on the pavement drawing. It'd make a great photo.

Before he's coloured his picture two slightly older lads tip up, one with a ball, the other with one arm in a sling.

"You're not the goalie, then?" I suggest.

"No, he is," he says, nodding to Mohammed, and the three of them go for a kick-about in the quiet street blocked off by the construction site.

THE REMAINS
OF MY KOBEDA KEBAB (SINGLE)
AT AL JAZEERA

I find myself in Today Fresh Shawarma on Grandale Street, just off the main road. It's been recommended by Haz, one of the brothers who run Mughli up the road. On his instructions I order a shawarma with pickled vegetables in the traditional samun bread. It's number one on the menu board.

"Next please!"

The Kebab meat is huge. It must take two of them to position it in front of the grill. "How long will that last?" I ask.

"Just today," says one of the staff as he makes up a pizza on the other side of the counter.

I finish my delicious Kebab and ask if I can sit and draw. My position on a high stool should be a good vantage point but this place is so busy I rarely get a clear view of the counter.

I'm jostled by customers on either side — this is extreme sketching — and, as the drawing develops, I attract attention.

Ahmed, from Saudi Arabia, has been in Manchester for two months. "Why you do this?" he asks. With the help of Google Translate and a young Iraqi lad sitting on the other side, I explain I sketch as a way of storytelling. He's unconvinced, wipes his mouth, and leaves.

"Your English is very good," I say to the Iraqi lad who beams. Turns out he's in the UK to learn the language. Already he's spent time in Swansea and has been in Manchester for less than a week.

"What do you make of our city?"

"Better than Swansea," he says.

"Next please!"

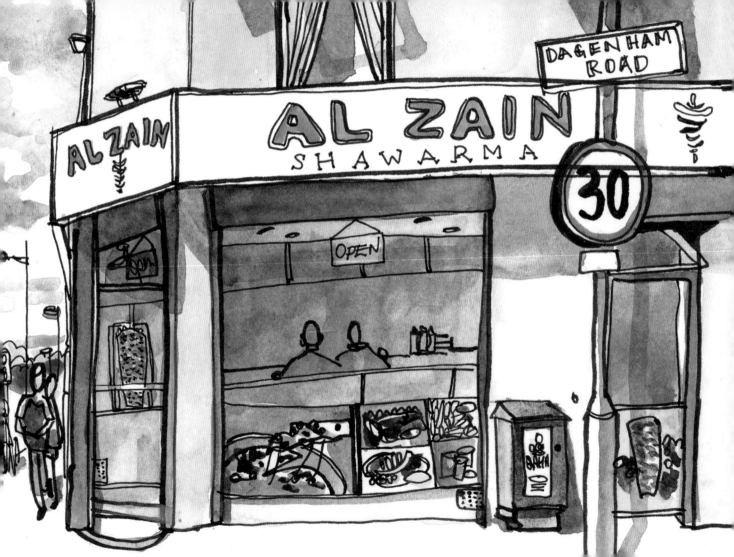

"The secret of our success? It's the quality. We're like Marks and Spencer. We always keep the quality very high. We use purified butter ghee which is tastier and has a good smell. It's better for you. That's the secret."

My old school, Xaverian College. It's been a sixth form college since I left.

3A, my first year classroom, was top left at Ward Hall (right).

At lunchtime a queue would snake round the back, past the smelly bins, to reach the dining room on the ground floor.

This is the ballroom at the iconic south Manchester nightclub Antwerp Mansion. "It was built in 1840 as part of the Victoria Park gated community for rich industrialists," Evie tells me, "and converted to a private members' club in 1922. Seven years ago it became Antwerp Mansion, the nightclub."

"And tell me about the ghosts," I say.

"The ghosts? We've been investigated by several paranormal societies who've all reported 'good activity', although I don't know whether I'm a believer myself."

Mohammed's father is now in his 90s but apparently still recalls having to pay a shilling toll to get through the gates of Victoria Park into what was then a private estate.

"Back then Rusholme had some nice shops: hat shops, sherbet shops, catering for the wealthy people who lived nearby. Now, of course, it's become much more commercialised."

"Is business more challenging nowadays?" I ask before I set up to draw from the other side of the cycle lane.

"There's more competition with the big superstores, but we've got our own select clientele. Some families have been coming to our shop for 40 years. We're known for our quality and being able to source the right produce for our customers."

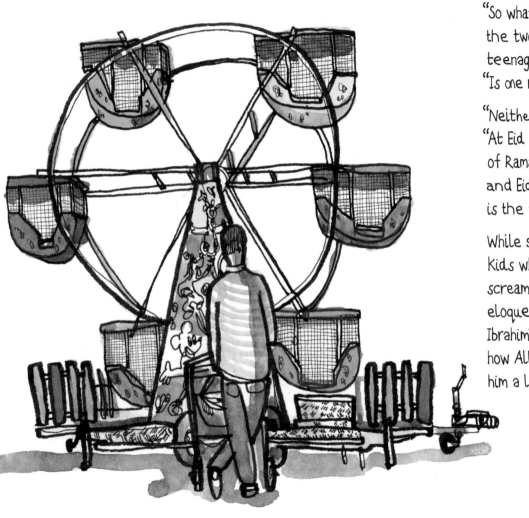

"So what's the difference between the two Eids?" I ask Ayshah, a teenage helper at Eid in the Park. "Is one more important?"

"Neither is more important," she says, "At Eid al-Fitr we celebrate the end of Ramadan, the month of fasting, and Eid al-Adha, which is more holy, is the festival of sacrifice."

While she shepherds four young kids whose older siblings are screaming on the Mexican Wave, she eloquently explains the story of Ibrahim's sacrifice of his son and how Allah, at the last minute, gave him a lamb to sacrifice instead.

LATIF THE RUSHOLME BUTCHER

"Yes, everyone ordered lamb for Eid. Whole sheep, 27 or 28 Kilos each. Altogether we sold 45 on the day and I prepared them all there on that table."

"How long have you been in the business?"

"All my life," Poonam laughs. "My dad started the business 41 years ago in 1977. We've been in three locations in Rusholme since then.

"Me and my brother are keen to do more online and invest in social media but my parents are just happy to open up and serve whoever walks in. That's the way it is."

The family has been trading in Rusholme for 30 years. First with a halal meat store, then a newsagent. "And five years ago the second generation came up with the idea for a grill bar and dessert café," Sunny tells me, "and so we opened this restaurant.

"Young people don't want to eat curries every day. They want snacky food like grills and burgers. And it has to look good for social media. They won't eat anything before taking a picture of it first."

"So you feel positive for the future of Rusholme?"

"Absolutely. Rusholme will never die. It's world famous. But we have to move with the times and give the customer what they want."

Sunny comes back with a Jilani's menu. "That's our logo," he says, hopefully.

Thanks to: (in order of appearance)

Kurdish Barbers; Afghan Cuisine Café; Delhi Sweet House; Shisha House; Rusholme Chippy; Manchester Central Mosque; Kurdistan Restaurant; Chunkyz; Jaffa; Antalya; The Pastry House; Atlas Shawarma; Al Medina; Bicycle Doctor; Albert Inn; Dubai Café; Junaid Jamshed by Janan; Mughli; Istanbul Turkish Cuisine; Al Jazeera; Today Fresh Shawarma; Anchor Coffee House; Sanam; Al-Noor Jewellers; Fancy Jewellers; Xaverian College; Antwerp Mansion; Jilani's; Manchester Super Store; Alankar House of Sarees; Ravi Food Store; Kurdish Barbers ...

.... and everyone who's stopped by for a chat.